AF131418

BOOK ANALYSIS

By Benjamin Taylor

Pale Fire

by Vladimir Nabokov

**Shed new light
on your favorite books with**

Bright
≡**Summaries**.com

www.brightsummaries.com

VLADIMIR NABOKOV

RUSSIAN-AMERICAN NOVELIST

- **Born in St. Petersburg in 1899.**
- **Died in Montreux in 1977.**
- **Notable works:**
  - *Lolita* (1955), novel
  - *Pnin* (1957), novel
  - *Ada or Ardor: A Family Chronicle* (1969), novel

Born into an aristocratic Russian family in the late 19th century, Vladimir Nabokov would go on to become one of the foremost novelists of the 20th century. His family were forced to flee Russia after the 1917 October Revolution and he lived in Paris and Berlin as an exile, before moving to America in reaction to the looming danger of German occupation of France in the Second World War (1939-45) during the early 1940s. Nabokov was a renowned linguist, able to speak Russian, English and French fluently. He began writing in Russian, but it was not until he took up English – with novels such as the revered but controversial *Lolita* – that he began to achieve commercial and critical success. Nabokov is generally associated with innovative experiments with structure and plot, as well as with linguistic prowess, his prose boasting an elaborate use of metaphors, puns and stylish lyricism. Nabokov is the author of dozens of novels, short stories, poems and plays and was, in his time, also well regarded as an entomologist, becoming an expert in the study of butterflies.

PALE FIRE

A POEM IN HEROIC COUPLETS

- **Genre:** novel
- **Reference edition:** Nabokov, V. (2000) *Pale Fire*. London: Penguin Classics.
- **1st edition:** 1962
- **Themes:** literature, America, outsiderdom, metafiction, criticism, fantasy, authorship

Pale Fire was published in 1962 and consists of a 999-line poem said to be the masterwork of the fictional poet John Shade, and a set of accompanying notes and commentary by Charles Kinbote, his colleague, neighbour and one-time editor. Kinbote is unreliable and seemingly on the brink of madness, claiming to be the exiled king of a fictional country named Zembla. Though he starts out with critical intentions, his commentary veers into wild and fantastical tales of his life, apparent friendship with Shade and self-obsessed readings of the poem. Set largely in the fictional college town of New Wye, the book displays the vast stylistic power of Nabokov's prose and poetry alike, as well as the ingenuity he is known for in his treatment of literary form. The novel contains references to several of the author's other works, including the appearance of a storm named 'Lolita' (a reference to his novel of the same name) and the recurring character of Professor Pnin, the protagonist of the 1957 novel *Pnin*. Despite being one of Nabokov's lesser-known works, *Pale Fire* is widely regarded as one of the finest works of literature of the 20th century, and the novel which cemented his place as the preeminent literary figure of his time.

SUMMARY

FOREWORD

The novel starts with a foreword by the poem's editor, Charles Kinbote, who reveals his own relationship to the poet and the difficulty he encountered in gaining the editorial rights to the poem following the death of its author, John Shade. Kinbote claims to have moved into a house next door to the celebrated poet upon getting a job in a university and to have befriended him and his wife quite by accident, though his account of the circumstances of their burgeoning friendship appears to be embellished and warped by his strange and sometimes obsessive manner. With this in mind, Kinbote tells of the jealousy of other faculty members and critics and concludes by stipulating the proper use of his commentary and the importance of the criticism in tandem with the poem itself.

PALE FIRE BY JOHN SHADE

In Canto One, Shade ruminates on his child-hood, the first part of which was dotted with illness, and his formative experiences with the nature of death and dying and the supernatural. This is followed by the Second Canto, in which he contemplates the question of existence after death, before providing snapshots into his family life, with his wife and daughter, Hazel. Hazel was unfortunate enough to inherit the same cosmetic disadvantages as her father, and as such had trouble fitting in well at school. She was stood up by a blind date in 1957 and found drowned in a lake the next day, though the cause of death remains unknown. In the Third Canto, Shade grieves and talks of working at what he calls the I.P.H. (Institute of Preparation for the Hereafter), where he talks of his journey into attempting to understand whether an afterlife exists. Though he is at first pessimistic, during a near-death experience (a heart attack) Shade sees a white fountain, something which he believes to be linked with the afterlife. He reads of a woman having had a similar experience, though on meeting her he discovers that there was a misprint of 'mountain' in the article. He leaves, nevertheless with what he calls a "faint hope" (p. 53). In the final canto, Shade defines his relationship to poetry and art in general when broadly understanding his existence. The poem ends abruptly, halfway through a rhyming couplet, the implication being that it is unfinished.

COMMENTARY BY CHARLES KINBOTE

Kinbote then launches into his commentary, analysing individual sections of text in an apparent critical appraisal of the poem. He begins to deviate drastically from this mission, however, launching instead into the story of King Charles Xavier, the last king of Zembla (a fictional place described as "a northern land" (p. 248)) who was exiled after a revolutionary coup. Kinbote recounts in great detail how King Charles was barricaded in the palace following the revolution, only to escape with the help of his friend and loyal royalist Odon through a secret passage known to them during their childhood days. He travels across the country and manages to escape Zembla altogether by boat.

Kinbote intertwines this narrative with further descriptions of his relationship with John Shade and how, having found out about his supposedly 'great' friend's creative endeavour, he took to spying on him from the convenience of the next-door window. Kinbote talks with an increasingly jealous propriety about critical ownership of Shade's work, believing that their friendship gives him the right to have the authoritative say about its meaning.

Meanwhile, King Charles has fled with Odon to Paris. Kinbote describes the emergence of Gradus, a radical, zealous but incompetent leftist revolutionary in Zembla tasked with assassinating the King. He travels to Paris in search of him, at the same time, as Kinbote claims, as Shade began writing the Second Canto of *Pale Fire*. In the commentary on this Second Canto, Kinbote continues with his narrative of Gradus, who widens his search for the King, and comments on Shade's reflections about his daughter's death. Around this time, King Charles, who is homosexual, was coerced into marrying for the purpose of fathering an heir – the unfortunate woman being Queen Disa. Kinbote describes the difficulties the King has settling into his marriage and continues to decry the lack of oblique reference to the story of King Charles in Shade's poem, instead making wild leaps about its subtext.

Around the time of John Shade's heart attack, we learn that King Charles – who, it is revealed, is in fact Kinbote himself – arrives in America, having left his wife in order to teach Zemblan at Wordsmith College. Gradus, meanwhile, has arrived in Nice and is awaiting instruction as to the whereabouts of his prey. Kinbote continues to refer sections of text to what he claims are draft lines of poetry, as well as conversations he has apparently written down between him and Shade – including one concerning the nature of God and the afterlife. Kinbote had become increasingly eager to read the poem, which he believed was enriched by the tale of the exile of King Charles Xavier (i.e. the character who we are supposed to believe is him). It is on the day Shade has granted him access to the poem that the poet meets his end, as Gradus arrives in New Wye, having found out King Charles' location. He is described travelling to the university and accessing his address from a student. As Shade and Kinbote are walking to the poet's house, Gradus opens fire, killing John Shade accidentally while trying to hit Kinbote. Upon reading the poem, Kinbote is dismayed to find nothing of his beloved Zembla. He coerces Shade's window into granting him sole editorial rights, and interviews Gradus, who later kills himself in prison. The novel ends with a long index written by Kinbote.

CHARACTER STUDY

JOHN SHADE

John Shade was the celebrated author of the poem *Pale Fire*, and before his untimely death lived in the town of New Wye with his wife Sybil and worked at Wordsmith University. Much of what we discover about John Shade comes from Charles Kinbote, the editor of his final poem who claims to have been a good friend of his and who is at times enraptured by his genius. Charles remembers that his physical appearance was generally untended to, so focussed was the poet on intellectual pursuits: "his misshapen body, that grey mop of abundant hair, the yellow nails of his pudgy fingers, the bags under his lustreless eyes, were only intelligible if regarded as the waste products eliminated from his intrinsic self by the same forces of perfection which purified and chiselled his verse" (p. 23). Indeed, as the novel progresses, we find two versions of John: the John of his own autobiographical poem, *Pale Fire*, and the John remembered and obsessed over by Kinbote, whose ultimate dream is for John to enshrine the life and exile of Charles Xavier, the last king of the fictional Zembla, in his celebrated verse. While the John of Charles' memories seems highly embellished and caricature-like in an attempt to demonstrate the fullness of their friendship, the author of *Pale Fire* is deeply reflective, still grieving the premature death of his daughter, Hazel, and in a life-long artistic investigation as to the nature of life after death. He appears, by the end of the poem, to have gladly reached an agnostic viewpoint on this issue, writing: "I have returned convinced that I can grope // My way to some – to some – 'Yes dear?' Faint hope" (p. 53, lines 833-4). He met his end, if we are to believe Kinbote, at the hands of an assassin named Gradus, who in his incompetency shot and killed the poet while trying to kill Kinbote himself.

CHARLES KINBOTE

Charles Kinbote, a native Zemblan who lived next door to John Shade in New Wye and taught his native language at the university, appears in *Pale Fire* as the editor of the poem, having retrieved the rights to do so from Shade's still-grieving widow. Much of the novel is made up of his own notes, commentary and reflections on the poem and its author, so much so that his supposed criticism begins to dominate it. He is eccentric, homosexual, apparently disliked by much of the faculty and obsessive about John Shade and his upcoming work, spying on him through his window in an attempt to create a timeline of the completion of the various sections and constantly asserting the power and importance of their friendship: "the thick venom of envy began squirting at me as soon as academic suburbia realized that John Shade valued my society above that of all other people" (p. 22). It is however implied by Mrs Shade's dislike of him, John's avoidance of him and the absence of him from Shade's work or subsequent obituaries that this friendship is highly exaggerated.

In the novel, Charles deviates from his critical operation in his commentary by telling us the highly detailed and fantastical story of the exiled King Charles Xavier, the last king of Zembla, who, if we are to believe everything he tells us, is Charles Kinbote himself under the guise of a false identity. Charles is desperate that his story should be commemorated in verse by the great poet John Shade. He is then dismayed that there appears to be no reference to the story in the poem, and instead makes wild assumptions about vague references. It is apparent that he faces exile yet again, writing his critical commentary to *Pale Fire* from the fictional town of Cedarn due to mistrust surrounding his actions after John's death, having been "forced to leave New Wye soon after my last interview with the jailed killer" (p. 16).

KING CHARLES XAVIER (A.K.A. CHARLES KINBOTE)

King Charles is the last king of Zembla, a fictional country described only as "a distant northern land" (p. 248) in the index of the novel. Though this is revealed to be the true identity of Charles Kinbote, questions surrounding the reliability of his narration and the fantastical nature of the story of King Charles seem to separate the two into distinct characters. King Charles is said to have become "passionately addicted to the study of literature" (p. 63) in his native land and is recognised by "the straight rugged frame, the erect carriage, the high-bridged nose, the straight brow, and the energetic arm swing" (p. 221). In the story, King Charles is ousted and imprisoned by a revolutionary group within Zembla, only to escape and live as an exile in Paris. Though he is homosexual, he was coerced into marrying, to end "his copious but sterile pleasures" (p. 139) in order to "take a night off and lawfully engender an heir" (*ibid.*). The marriage, for obvious reasons, did not last and the two separated, King Charles moving to America to teach at a university and become Charles Kinbote – whose name means regicide in Zemblan, reflecting the symbolic death of his kingship: "a king who sinks his identity in the mirror of exile is in a sense just that" (p. 210).

HAZEL SHADE

Hazel Shade is the daughter of John, and was found drowned in a lake in 1957 under mysterious circumstances. It was unknown whether she had committed suicide – having earlier in the night been stood up on a blind date – or whether it was something more sinister. Hazel is defined in the novel through the perspective of its two authors – her father, who appears to have been greatly affected by her death ("She was my darling: difficult, morose – // But still my darling" (p. 39, lines 357-8)), and Kinbote, who describes her with far less tact. She was unfortunate enough to inherit her father's looks, and as such grew up as an unpopular and strange girl: "the flabby, feeble, clumsy and solemn girl, who seemed more interested than frightened" (p. 134). Her death and its aftermath make up a large segment of the Second Canto of *Pale Fire*, with John Shade evidently still grieving her loss. She is furthermore described by Kinbote as having notably manufactured a number of supernatural events in her family home following the death of her Aunt Maud.

ANALYSIS

GENRE

Pale Fire, with its intricate and innovative construction, is often thought of as a piece of metafiction: i.e. a work of fiction that acknowledges its artificiality and the nature of its creation. We find this in the multiple layers of authorship present in the novel, with the poem itself commentated on by a critic (Charles Kinbote) and all the text written by Nabokov himself. Throughout the novel the reader is aware that the poem and its poet are fictionalised, as is the critic, meaning that Nabokov is effectively commentating on his own work, or at least artificially recreating the process of criticism. As such, the truth about authorship and the reality of the various intertwining stories within the novel can be called into question, particularly due to the unreliability of the editor Charles Kinbote. We do not know, for example, whether Charles is who he says he is, given the fantastical nature of his story about the exiled King Charles Xavier. It might also be the case that the fictional Charles Kinbote has himself penned the poem *Pale Fire*, inventing the author John Shade in order to use it as device to tell his story. By drawing attention to the fictional nature of the novel, Nabokov allows us to question the nature of authorship, the reliability of storytelling and the uncertainty of fiction. As such, it is difficult to ascertain any truth in *Pale Fire* other than the knowledge that what we are reading is constructed. This is of course exacerbated by the fictional nature of both the characters and the places they inhabit, including the imagined American college town of New Wye and the country of Zembla.

OUTSIDERDOM AND FOREIGNNESS

As with many of Nabokov's other works, the theme of foreignness and exile are prevalent in *Pale Fire*, with the isolated central character of Charles Kinbote resembling the central characters of several Nabokov protagonists. Charles is, in particular, an exile on two separate levels, having retreated to the remote and fictional American town of Cedarn following his unmannerly actions in the wake of the death of John

Shade, and in line with his concealed identity as Charles Xavier, the last king of Zembla who is forced to flee his native land as a result of a revolution. Charles strikes an isolated figure in the course of his commentary, apparently unpopular with his fellow staff, blatantly disliked by Sybil Shade and actively avoided by his supposed 'friend' John. He is perhaps treated as such both because of his eccentricity and because of his foreignness, character traits present, for example, in Nabokov's works *Lolita* – a novel told from the perspective of a French paedophile in America – and *Pnin* which, like Kinbote in *Pale Fire*, details the life of a Russian émigré working in a small-town American college. Indeed, the central character of *Pnin*, Timofey Pnin, appears in *Pale Fire* as a seldom-referenced and ridiculed member of the Wordsmith University teaching staff.

The isolation caused by emigration is of course something that Nabokov would have experienced himself, having been forced to flee his native Russia following the Bolshevik Revolution of 1917. Indeed, the journey of Nabokov's exile reflects that of the fictional King Charles, who was likewise forced from his native land by social revolution and lived in Europe (Nabokov lived in Berlin for over a decade) before settling in America to teach at an American university. It is likely that this recurring character trait is indicative of an autobiographical strain prevalent in Nabokov's writing.

STYLE

Pale Fire is of course made up not just of the eponymous poem, but of a foreword, critical commentary and index. In other words, all parts generally associated with published poetry are fictionalised by Nabokov in the creation of something that is neither prose nor poetry. Indeed, it is difficult to define *Pale Fire* – containing elements of poetry, critical accompaniment and prose – and instead it seems to resemble the fictional recreation of a literary artefact. The poem itself is written in heroic couplets, which are couplets (pairs of end-rhymed lines) written in iambic pentameter (a metre commonly used by Shakespeare in his sonnets). Heroic couplets are historically used in epic poetry, in particular by English writers such as Geoffrey Chaucer, who pioneered its literary use in the 14th century, and Alexander Pope, who used it extensively in the 18th century. The use of this literary device gives the poetry a gravitas, associated with its historical use, elevating John Shade's poem to a piece of work which transcends historical boundaries. The amalgamation of the foreword, commentary and index, while apparently resembling traditional aspects of literary appraisal, are used by Nabokov – and unknowingly by the editor Charles Kinbote – as a space in which to develop what seems like a short novel, which tells the story of King Charles Xavier and of John Shade himself. Nabokov's use of literary form in *Pale Fire* is therefore multifaceted in the creation of a rich and diverse storytelling technique.

CRITICISM

Nabokov, as one of *the* preeminent writers of the 20th century, was of course no stranger to the practice and effects of literary criticism. In *Pale Fire* he addresses the nature of this sort of criticism fully by writing a fictional appraisal of one of his own poems (albeit written by a fictional character). The character of the critic, or rather editor, Charles Kinbote is, however, seemingly more concerned with himself than the literature that he is critiquing, dominating the commentary section with the story of his own life, his own gripes and exaggerations about his friendship with the author. He furthermore puts increasing importance on his own opinion in relation to the poem, claiming that "without my notes Shade's text simply has no human reality at all" (p. 25) and that "it is the commentator who has the last word" (*ibid*.). This is perhaps a pastiche of the act of criticism and critics themselves in that Kinbote actively attempts to find his own influence in the poem and is dismayed when there is little to work with. After attempting to coerce John Shade into including the tale of his own exile from Zembla, he says when he finds nothing: "the final text of *Pale Fire* has been deliberately and drastically drained of every trace of the material I contributed" (p. 67), desperately trying to find subtext ("that dim distant music, those vestiges of color in the air" (p. 233)) in order to justify the telling of his long-winded tale. He is even half-conscious of his own self-obsession, claiming to "have no desire to twist and batter an unambiguous *apparatus criticus* into the monstrous semblance of a novel" (p. 71), before going on to do just that. We are led to conclude, due to the often-ambiguous nature of poetry and its meaning, that criticism is intensely subjective, symbolism easily identified. Nabokov furthermore twists our perspective concerning the nature of criticism – using meta-fictional devices, in turning the supposed critic (Kinbote) into an author in himself – as though in performing literary criticism, writers are in fact creating fictions of their own.

FURTHER REFLECTION

SOME QUESTIONS TO THINK ABOUT...

- Nabokov is well-known for his playful linguistic style. How do you think the way Nabokov writes differs from other writers?
- How much of Charles Kinbote's commentary can we believe? Is he a reliable narrator to the second half of the novel?
- What do you think is the main story of *Pale Fire*? Is it the poem or the commentary? Does Kinbote's commentary overshadow the poem itself?
- What do you think Nabokov is trying to say about criticism? How does Kinbote's role as the critic change as the novel goes on?
- Consider the innovative form of the novel. How does *Pale Fire* differ from other novels you have studied?
- To what extent is *Pale Fire* autobiographical? How much of his own life does the author insert into his work?

- Though probably Nabokov's most critically revered work, *Pale Fire* is far less well-known than his novel *Lolita*. Why do you think this is?
- Outside of the context of the novel as a whole, how can we approach the poem itself in a critical sense? Is the poem just a device through which Nabokov is able to reveal the character of Kinbote?

We want to hear from you!
Leave a comment on your online library
and share your favourite books on social media!

FURTHER READING

REFERENCE EDITION

- Nabokov, V. (2000) *Pale Fire*. London: Penguin Classics.

MORE FROM BRIGHTSUMMARIES.COM

- Reading guide – *Lolita* by Vladimir Nabokov.
- Reading guide – *Pnin* by Vladimir Nabokov.

Bright ≡Summaries.com

BOOK ANALYSIS

More guides to rediscover your love of literature

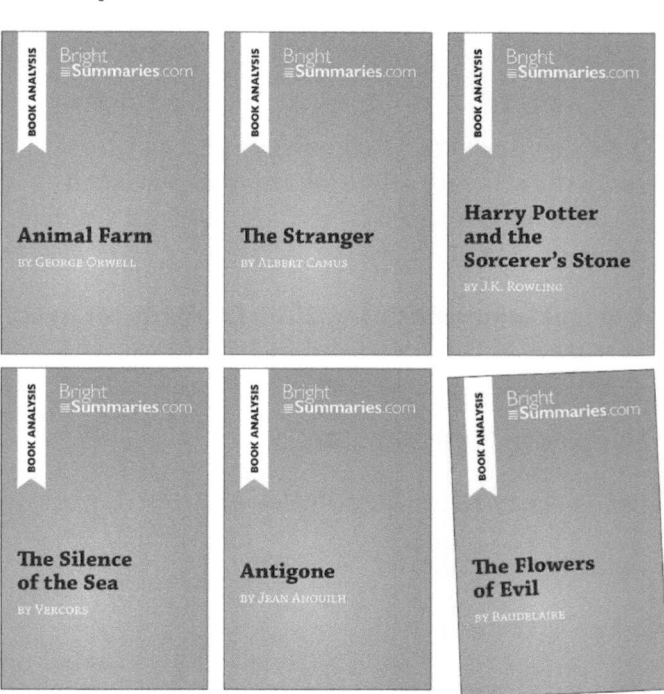

Animal Farm
BY GEORGE ORWELL

The Stranger
BY ALBERT CAMUS

Harry Potter and the Sorcerer's Stone
BY J.K. ROWLING

The Silence of the Sea
BY VERCORS

Antigone
BY JEAN ANOUILH

The Flowers of Evil
BY BAUDELAIRE

www.brightsummaries.com

Although the editor makes every effort to verify the accuracy of the information published, BrightSummaries.com accepts no responsibility for the content of this book.

© BrightSummaries.com, 2019. All rights reserved.

www.brightsummaries.com

Ebook EAN: 9782808019743

Paperback EAN: 9782808019750

Legal Deposit: D/2019/12603/154

Cover: © Primento

Digital conception by Primento, the digital partner of publishers.